Faith
By John Owen
Edited by Cameron Dula

© 2021 by Cameron Dula

Published by: H&E Publishing, Peterbourough, Ontario
www.hesedandemet.com

All rights reserved. This book or any portion thereof may not be reproduced or used in any manner whatsoever without the express written permission of the publisher except for the use of brief quotations in a book review.

John Owen, *The Works of John Owen*, vol. 9 (Edinburgh: T. & T. Clark, 1862).

Scripture quotations are from The ESV® Bible (The Holy Bible, English Standard Version®), copyright © 2001 by Crossway, a publishing ministry of Good News Publishers. Used by permission. All rights reserved.

Cover painting: *Syria by the Sea* by Frederic Edwin Church

Design and layout: Dustin Benge

Paperback ISBN: 978-1-77484-004-7
EBook ISBN: 978-1-77484-005-4

First edition, 2021

FAITH
Steadfast in Trials

JOHN OWEN

Edited by Cameron Dula

CONTENTS

Biography: The Life and Ministry of John Owen		7
Preface		13
1	The Strength of Faith	17
2	The Use of Faith in a Time of Public Calamity	51
3	The Use of Faith Under Persecution	67
4	The Use of Faith Under Anti-Christian Rulers	81
5	The Use of Faith in a Time of General Decline	93

"The apostles said to the Lord,

'Increase our faith!'"

LUKE 17:5

BIOGRAPHY

The Life and Ministry of John Owen

John Owen was born in 1616 to Puritan parents in the town of Stadhampton in Oxfordshire. Proving to be a gifted student under the tutelage of his father, Henry, Owen seems to have made quick progress in academia, and was admitted to the Queen's College, Oxford at twelve years of age. Owen was a diligent and disciplined learner, allowing himself no more than four hours of sleep each night so that he might amass more knowledge. A practice he would learn to regret in later years as he realized that those late nights spent reading and studying had come at the price of his health. Suffering from varied health issues throughout his life, Owen was even hindered at times from preaching. On June 11, 1632, Owen was awarded his B.A. and his M.A. on April 27, 1635, at nineteen years of age. At this point in his life, Owen does not seem to have been deeply affected by the power of God's Word, aiming instead to work ardently to obtain a position of honor for himself. Thankfully, the Scripture reminds us that, "Many are the plans in the mind of a man, but it is the purpose of the LORD that will stand" (Prov. 19:21). God was preparing and equipping his wayward child to spend his days extolling the riches of Christ in ways that he could not have imagined.

The Balm of the Gospel

After leaving university in 1637, Owen entered a season of serious struggle in his soul. During this season, he withdrew himself, avoided socializing, and rarely ever spoke, or when he did speak, it was said that there was little coherence in his words. One day, while living in the Charter House, he and his cousin decided to hear Edmund Calamy (1600–1666) at St. Mary's Church, Aldermanbury. Calamy was a prestigious Presbyterian minister and the obvious power that accompanied his preaching drew people from far and wide. However, for an unexplained reason, the day Owen decided to attend, Calamy was unable to preach. As this news spread, many in the church began to leave. A friend urged Owen to do the same so that they might hear another distinguished scholar and notable preacher at another church by the name of Arthur Jackson (c. 1593–1666). Owen refused to leave and remained in his seat at St. Mary's. An unknown country preacher entered the pulpit, offered a prayer, and read his text. "Why are you afraid, O you of little faith?" (Matt. 8:26). The glorious truth gripped his soul, and John Owen, after a half-decade of turmoil, felt the healing balm of the gospel applied to his soul. Owen was set ablaze by an all-consuming zeal for God. A zeal that flowed from personal knowledge of Christ revealed in the gospel.

A Life of Ministry

Later that year, in 1642, John Owen published his first work, *A Display of Arminianism*. This work extols salvation as a work of God alone, which laid the groundwork and set the trajectory for Owen's future ministry. In 1643, Owen was called to a pastorate in the village of Fordham and remained there until 1646 when he became the minister of the church at Coggeshall. It is recorded that as many as two thousand people would hear Owen preach each Lord's Day. This same period, Owen shifted his understanding of church government from Presbyterianism to Congregationalism after reading *The Keyes of the Kingdom of Heaven* by John Cotton (1584–1652). While at Coggeshall he penned what has become perhaps his most famous work, *The Death of Death in the Death of Christ* published in 1647.

By the early 1650's, Owen had developed a close friendship with Oliver Cromwell (1599–1658) and eventually

FAITH

became one of his closest advisors regarding matters of the church and state. Cromwell appointed Owen to Vice Chancellor of Oxford University in 1652 where he reorganized the faculty and ministered to students through lectures and preaching. During these fruitful years, Owen wrote *The Mortification of Sin in Believers* published in 1656. However, in 1656, when it was suggested that Cromwell assume the monarchy, Owen strongly advised against it, and though Cromwell refused the crown, irreputable damage was done to their friendship.

Longing for Glory

Owen spent the last decade of his life offering counsel to those who came to him seeking advice. In the final hours before his death, Owen wrote to a dear friend, Charles Fleetwood (c. 1618–1692), informing him that he was "going to Him whom his soul loved and that all of his consolations was wholly grounded in the everlasting love of Christ for him." The next day he was visited by a fellow minister, William Payne (c. 1648–1726), who came to inform Owen that his meditations on the glory of Christ were going to press that very hour. Owen replied that he was glad to hear it but that the day he had long wished for had come at last—he would soon see the glory he wrote about in ways that he was incapable of in this world. He had spent his life seeking to behold and holding forth this glory to others but now was going face to face with his

Lord. John Owen entered that glory on August 24, 1683.

Owen's legacy is immense and can not be overstated. His sermons, treatises, and other words continue to inform students of Scripture on the subjects of glory, sin, and the Christian life. John Owen stands as a towering figure of colossal intelligence and humble godliness.

"Because of your little faith. For truly, I say to you, if you have faith like a grain of mustard seed, you will say to this mountain, 'Move from here to there,' and it will move, and nothing will be impossible for you."

MATTHEW 17:20

PREFACE

Cameron Dula

On his deathbed, John Owen instructed his secretary to pen a letter to a friend in his name. Owen instructed him to write, "I am still in the land of the living." However, Owen had an abrupt realization, "Stop! Change that and say, I am yet in the land of the dying, but I hope soon to be in the land of the living." This vividly illustrates the life of faith Owen lived. During his funeral sermon, the minister lamented the loss of Owen by saying, "We have lost an excellent pilot, and lost him when a fierce storm is coming upon us when we have most need of him." Extracted from his sermons on the church, Owen serves as an excellent pilot to navigate the subject of faith lived out in the Christian life.

Though preached in the seventeenth-century, Owen's

FAITH

sermons on the church could not be more applicable to our present day. Masterfully theological and thoroughly biblical, Owen details our security in Christ and our duty towards him. He writes, "Though you take a weak and faint hold on Christ, he takes a sure, strong, and unconquerable hold on you." Such a glorious truth resembles the comforting words of Christ, "My sheep hear my voice, and I know them, and they follow me. I give them eternal life, and they will never perish, and no one will snatch them out of my hand" (John 10:27–28). Owen reminds believers that there are no alternate routes for faithfully living the Christian life, but that "the righteous shall live by faith" (Hab. 2:4).

Owen highlights two specific works that faith performs within a believer. First, faith empties the soul of the self. In other words, true faith reveals the utter emptiness, insufficiency, and nothingness that we have for spiritual ends. Faith is vitally essential if believers are to live lives pleasing to Christ. Second, faith ushers the soul to God, moving a believer to give themselves up entirely to his sovereign disposal. If we are to live steadfastly by faith, it's paramount that we realize our inability to do so and our utter need to yield ourselves to God. With sensitive pastoral care and precision, Owen guides us into a rich understanding of what it means to have faith and to live by faith.

It is my earnest prayer, sincere desire, and confident hope that the Lord will use Owen to guide you to see

Steadfast in Trials

Christ more clearly in preparation for the seasons of calamity yet to be faced. James instructs, "Count it all joy, my brothers, when you meet trials of various kinds, for you know that the testing of your faith produces steadfastness. And let steadfastness have its full effect, that you may be perfect and complete, lacking in nothing" (James 1:2–4). May the Lord be pleased to make these words the experience of all his children as they seek to live by faith, steadfast in trials.

"No unbelief made him waver concerning the promise of God, but he grew strong in his faith as he gave glory to God."

ROMANS 4:20

ONE

The Strength of Faith

In this chapter the apostle singles out a notable example in order to make good the conclusion which he had proved in the previous chapter by various convincing demonstrations. Namely, that the justification of a sinner could not be brought about but by the righteousness of faith in Christ. I say this in the example of Abraham and from the testimonies given concerning him and the way he was justified before God. The apostle proves this from the beginning of the chapter to the end of verse seventeen. From there to the end of verse twenty-two he describes that faith of Abraham by which he obtained acceptance with God, that in all things he might propose him as an example and an encouragement to us.

Among the many excellencies which are given in the

description of this faith of his, arising from its cause, object, matter, and manner not now to be insisted on, this is none of the least which is mentioned, "No unbelief made him waver." That is, he was steadfast in believing or as it is expounded in the close of the verse, "He grew strong in his faith." These words may yield us these two observations. First, all wavering at the promises of God is through unbelief. The apostle says, "No unbelief made him waver." Men are apt to pretend many other reasons and do use other pleas, but the truth is that all our wavering is through unbelief. Another proposition lies in the text and that is what I will now apply myself unto. Second, steadfastness in believing the promises is exceedingly acceptable unto God. In treating this subject, I will do these two things: 1. Explain the terms of the proposition, and 2. Give the proof of it.

Faith and Steadfastness Explained

As to the former of these there is the object concerning which the affirmation is laid down which is the promises of God. The promises of God are the declaration of the purposes of his grace towards his elect according to the terms of the covenant. That pointed unto was the old great promise of Christ which contains in it all others, "For all the promises of God find their yes in him" (2 Cor. 1:20). So that although I will speak nothing but what will be true with reference to every promise of God whatsoever, yet I will bear a chief respect to the promises that exhibit Christ and the free grace of God in him unto sinners and steadfastness in believing these promises.

There is the act that is exercised about this object and that is, believing. It is steadfastness in believing I speak of. It is not my intention to discuss the nature of faith or to debate the differences that are among men about it. Only so much as may give us an acquaintance with the subject we are treating. How many have been the disputes of men about the nature of faith? The subject, proper object, and formal reason of faith? And how little the church of God is revealing to men who have made it their business to involve things of general duty and absolute necessity unto all believers in intricate disputes? Those that will duly consider it may easily know. By some men understanding too much, others are brought to understand nothing at all. He that would have the things of his own spiritual experience and daily duty made unintelligible to him, let him consider them as stated in men's philosophical disputes about them. Some place faith in one distinct faculty of the soul, some in another, and some say there are no such thing as distinct faculties in the soul. Some place it in both the chief faculties, namely, the understanding and the will. Some say it is impossible that one habit should have its residence in two faculties. My intention is to speak principally to such as God chooses, the poor and foolish of the world and the means he will employ to bring them to himself are not, I am sure, above that understanding which the Son of God has given them (1 John 5:20). And whereas the general way in treating faith is, for the most part, to use strictness of expression, that it may be delivered in a philosophical exactness, the constant way of the Holy Ghost is by metaphorical expressions. Adaptations of it to things of sense and daily usage in the meanest in order to give a savor and perception of it to all that are interested in it. I will labor to speak that every one that does believe may know what it is to believe. Only observe that I speak of believing and of faith in respect of that end and to that purpose only. In reference to how Paul here treats it, which is in respect of justification and our acceptance with God.

So, I say that faith or believing in this restrained sense does not consist solely in the assent of the mind to the truth of the promises or of any promise. When one affirms anything to us and we say we believe him then we mean that the thing he speaks is true. There is this assent of the mind. Without this there is no faith, but this alone is not the faith we speak of. This alone and solitary the devils have and cannot choose but have it (James 2:19). They believe that which makes them tremble on the authority of God who reveals it. But you will say, "The devil believes only the threats of God and that which makes him tremble and so his belief is not a general assent but partial. And is thereby distinguished from our assent which is to all that

God has revealed and especially the promises." I answer that the devil believes the promises no less than he does the threats of God. That is that they are true and will be accomplished. Part of his misery is that he cannot but believe them and the promises of God are as much suited to make him tremble as his threatening's. The first promise to us was couched in a threat to him and there is no promise wherein a threat to him is not couched (Gen. 3:15). And there is no promise wherein a threat to him is not couched. Every word concerning Christ or grace by him speaks his downfall and ruin. Indeed, his destruction lies more in promises than threats. Promises are what weakens him daily and gives him a continual foretaste of his approaching destruction.

On this consideration it is evident that believing or faith cannot be solely an assent to the truth of these promises upon the fidelity of the promiser, but it is originally. Hence it is called receiving the testimony of God and therein setting to our seal that God is true (John 3:33). However, there is something more in receiving the testimony of God and setting our seal to it (agreeing as in contracts that it is so and that it will be so) than the bare assent of the mind to the truth of the promises. Although in ordinary speech, to receive a man's testimony is no more than to believe what he says, there seems to be an explanation in the annexed expression of setting our seal that is included when Job speaks, "Hear, and know it for your good" (Job

5:27). There is a receiving of it for ourselves in those expressions which adds much to a bare assent. I say then that this assent is of faith though it is not faith and in saying that it is not justifying faith we do not deny but affirm it to be faith in general. The addition of a peculiar assent does not destroy the nature of a thing. Now faith in general is such an assent as has been described.

It is not in the sole consent of the will to close with the promise as containing that which is good and suitable. There is the matter of the promise to be considered in believing as well as the promise itself. Christ with his righteousness and benefits is, as it were, offered unto us therein. Therefore, by believing we are said to accept or to "receive reconciliation" (Rom. 5:11). Now, to consent that the matter of the promise or that which is exhibited in the word is good and desirable and that it is so to us and to choose it on that account is required to believe also. And it is properly the receiving of Christ (John 1:12). However, it is not only precisely and exclusively this. Sarah's faith is described as, "she considered him faithful who had promised" (Heb. 11:11). This is of the nature of faith concerning considering him faithful that promises and assenting to the truth of his promises on that account. Now, the first of these may be without the second. Our assent may be without the consent of the will, but the latter cannot be without the former. But there is such an assent as will certainly produce this choice also.

Steadfast in Trials

I suppose I need not say it does not entirely consist in the desires of the affections and embracing the things promised. The stony ground received the word presently and with joy (Matt. 13:20). It is said that the seed sprung up immediately because it "had no depth of soil" (Matt. 13:5). Where men have warm affections but not thoroughly prepared minds and hearts they presently run away with the word and profess great matters from it. But where it is laid in deep, it is commonly longer before it appears. When a man receives the word only in the affections, the first touch of them cannot be hid. Instantly he will be speaking of it, melt under it, and declare how he is affected with it. Such as, "Oh, this sermon has done me good indeed!" Yet this is not faith when it is alone. They receive the word with joy but have not root in themselves (Matt. 13:20–21). When Christ promised, "The bread of life," that is, himself (John 6:35), how many were instantly affected with it and carried out to strong desires for it? They say, "Sir, give us this bread always" (John 6:34). They like it and they desire it at that season. Their affections are taken with it but they were only temporary. They were not true believers, for after a season they "turned back and no longer walked with him" (John 6:66). Do you not think that those "who have tasted the heavenly gift" (Heb. 6:4), like the taste and are affected with it? However, there are innumerable deceits in this business. When affections go before believing they are of little worth but when they follow it, they are

FAITH

exceedingly acceptable and precious in the sight of God.

It is not solely fiducia, that is, a trust or confidence. There is a twofold fiducial trust. One by which we trust in Christ for the forgiveness of sin, which you may call adherence. It is such a cleaving to Christ that we trust in him for the forgiveness of sins and acceptance with God. And so much as we trust, so much we adhere and no more. There is also a trust that our sins are forgiven and we trust or rest upon it. Now, it cannot be that either of these should be faith entirely or that the whole of it should be included in them. There is something more in believing than in trusting and something more in trusting than is absolutely necessary to preserve the entire notion of believing. For we may believe that wherein we do not trust but where there is believing in Christ there will also be trusting in him, more or less, and when faith is increased to some good height, strength, and steadfastness it is mainly taken up in trust and confidence (John 14:1). So, to believe as to free our hearts from trouble and unrest upon any account whatever is to trust properly and that doubting, staggering, and fear which we find condemned in Scripture as opposite to faith are indeed directly opposite to this fiduciary reposing our souls on Christ. This is how the apostle describes his faith or believing (2 Tim. 1:12). To believe as to be persuaded that God is able to keep what we commit to him is to put our trust in him.

Having spoken much of these particulars and waiving

all the arbitrary determinations of the schools and exactness of words as to philosophical rules and terms, I will give you such a general description of faith or believing that may answer in some measure the proper and metaphorical expressions of it in the Scriptures. There it is termed looking or seeing, hearing, tasting, resting, rolling ourselves upon, flying for refuge, and trusting.

Faith that God Accepts

There must be what I spoke of in the first place, an assent to the whole truth of the promises of God. Upon this ground and bottom, that he is able and faithful to accomplish his promises. This certainly is included in, if it is not all our receiving the testimony or witness of God (John 3:33). Sarah received the testimony of God and how did she do it? She "considered him faithful who had promised" (Heb. 11:11). God proposes this to us in the first place. Eternal life is promised by God who cannot lie (Titus 1:2). That is he who is so faithful as that it is utterly impossible that he should deceive any. "So, when God desired to show more convincingly to the heirs of the promise the unchangeable character of his purpose, he guaranteed it with an oath, so that by two unchangeable things, in which it is impossible for God to lie, we who have fled for refuge might have strong encouragement to hold fast to the hope set before us" (Heb. 6:17–18). The design of God is that we may receive encouragement in our fleeing for refuge to the hope

FAITH

set before us. Namely, in believing. What does he propose to this end? Why, his own faithfulness and immutability on the account of the engagement of his word and oath. Abraham's faith spoken of in Romans four comprises this and is commended for it (Rom. 4:21). The Scripture mentions various attributes of God that become the basis of our souls assenting and acquiesce to the truth of his promises owing to the credit his character, if I may say it that way.

Two especially are usually named. First, his power. He is able (Rom. 4:21; 11:23). Second, his faithfulness. As in the places before mentioned and various others. The sum is that on the account of God's faithfulness and power, this we are to do, if we will believe. We are to assent to the truth of his promises and the certainty of their accomplishment. If this is not done it is in vain to go forward. Let then those who intend any advantage by what will be spoken afterward stay here a little and consider how they have laid this foundation. There are many who never come to any stability all their days and yet are never able to fix on any certain cause of their shaking and staggering. The foundation was laid disorderly. This first closing with the faithfulness and power of God in the promises was never distinctly acted over in and by their souls and if the foundation be weak, let the building be ever so glorious, it will totter if not fall. Look then to this beginning of your confidence so that this does not fail you and when all other holds fail this will support you from utterly sinking if at any time you are reduced to that condition that you have nothing else.

Over and above this faith in the Scripture is expressed (and we find it by experience) to be the will's consent unto and acceptance of the Lord Jesus Christ as mediator. He that accomplished his work as the only way of going to the Father as the sole and sufficient cause of our acceptance with him and as our only righteousness before him. It has been said that faith is the receiving of Christ as a priest and a lord to be saved and ruled by him. This sounds excellent. Who is so vile that endeavoring to believe is not willing to be ruled by Christ as well as saved by him? A faith that would not have Christ to be Lord to rule us is that faith alone which James rejects. He that would be saved by Christ and not ruled by him will not be saved by him at all. We are to receive a whole Christ, not halves. We are to receive all of his offices not one or another.

This sounds well, makes a fair show, and there is truth in some regard in what is spoken but let men explain themselves and it comes to mean this. The receiving of Christ as a king is yielding obedience to him but that subjection is not a fruit of the faith whereby we are justified but an essential part of it. So that there is no difference between faith and works or obedience in the business of justification, both being an equal condition of it. When I recently read one saying that this was one principle that the Church of England went on in the Reformation and that faith and works have the same consideration in the business of justification, I could not help but stand amazed and conclude that either he or I had been asleep ever since we were born or that there were two Churches of England. One that I never knew and another that he never knew or else that prejudice is powerful and makes men confident. Is that the doctrine of the Church of England, as they call it? When, where, and by whom was it taught but by Papists and Socinians until recently in England? What place does it have in confessions, homilies, liturgies, controversy writers, or any other thing of repute for learning and religion in England? But this is no place for contest.

Others at length mince the matter and say that faith and works have the same respects to our justification that will be public and solemn at the last day, the day of judgment. And is this all that they have intended? How they will justify themselves at the day of judgment for troubling the peace of the saints of God and shaking the great fundamental articles of the Reformation, I do not know. It is true that faith receives Christ as a lord and as a king and it is no true faith that will not and does not do so and that does not put the soul upon all that obedience which he as the captain of our salvation requires at our hands. Yet faith, as it justifies, closes with Christ alone for righteousness and acceptance with God and it is in that act only, which is no less exclusive of good works than of sin. It closes with Christ in and for this on the account that he is our righteousness, for whom and by which we are justified.

But you will say, "This makes you Solifidians and are you not justly so accounted?" I say, Paul was a Solifidian, whose epistles will refute all the formalists and self-justiciaries in the world. We are Solifidians as to justification; Christ, grace, and faith are all. We are not Solifidians as to the entirety of salvation nor gospel conduct nor the declaration of the efficacy of our believing. Such Solifidians as exclude everything from an influence in our justification but our acceptance by the grace of God on the basis of faith's receiving of Christ for righteousness and salvation were all the apostles of Jesus Christ. Such Solifidians as exclude or deny the necessity of works and gospel obedience to him that is justified, or that say, a true and justifying faith may consist without holiness, works, and obedience are condemned by all the apostles and James in particular.

I say that receiving Christ is required of faith or believing. "His own people did not receive him" (John 1:11). The not receiving of Christ for such purposes as he is sent unto us by the Father is properly unbelief. Therefore, as it follows, the receiving him is properly faith or believing (John 1:12). So, in preaching the gospel we are said to make an offer or a presentation of Christ as the Scripture does (Rev. 22:17). Now, that which answers an offer or presentation is the acceptance of it. So that the soul's willing acceptance of the Lord Jesus Christ for our righteousness before God, being offered to us in the promises of the gospel for that end and purpose, from the love of the Father, is the main of that believing which is so acceptable unto God.

Add here to that which I cannot say is absolutely of the nature of faith but is in some degree or other (secret or more known to the soul) a necessary component of it and that is the soul's resting, quieting itself, and satisfying its affections in its interest in and enjoyment of a sweet, desirable Savior. This is called clinging to the Lord (Joshua 23:8). It is the fixing and fastening our affections on God as ours in covenant. This is the soul's resting in God. It is also the soul confiding and trusting in God. In these three things which are understandable to the poorest soul, written evidently in the words of the Scripture, and in the experience of those who have to do with God in Christ do I place the believing which is so acceptable to God.

Steadfast Faith

Next, there is the qualification of this believing as laid down in the proposition, which is steadfastness in believing. This is included in the negative. It is said of Abraham that, "He wavered not" (Rom. 4:21). That is, he was steadfast. To clear this up a little take these few observations.

Faith or believing consists in such a habitual frame of heart and such acting's of the soul as are capable of degrees, of straitening or enlargement, and of strength and weakness. This is why there is mention in the Scripture of great faith, "O woman, great is your faith" (Matt. 15:28). Of little faith, "O ye of little faith" (Matt. 6:30; 8:26; 16:8; Luke 12:28). Of strong faith, Abraham, "Grew strong in his faith" (Rom. 4:20). Of weak faith or being weak in faith, "The one who is weak in faith, welcome" (Rom.14:1). Of faith with doubting, "O you of little faith, why did you doubt" (Matt. 14:31). And of faith excluding doubting, "He grew strong in his faith" and "He wavered" or doubted not (Rom. 4:20).

That faith in every respect is equal as unto sincerity and only differs in degrees. It is equal in respect of the main effects and advance of it in justification, perseverance, and salvation. A little faith is no less faith than a great faith. Yea, a little faith will carry a man as safely to heaven as a great faith, though not as comfortably or fruitfully.

Steadfastness respects those different degrees of faith. It is not of the nature of faith but bespeaks such a degree of it as is acceptable to God that we should have and is in every way advantageous to ourselves. This is mentioned by Peter: "Take care that you are not carried away with the error of lawless people and lose your own stability" (2 Pet. 3:17), or decline from that stability in believing which you have attained. This is also mentioned by Paul (Col. 2:5).

There may be a true faith that may have many troublesome and perplexing doubts accompanying it, many sinful staggering's and wavering's attending it and yet not be overthrown but remain true faith. Men may be true

FAITH

believers and yet not strong believers. A child that eats milk has as truly the nature of a man as he that being grown up lives on strong meat. Now, steadfastness denotes stability in believing in respect of the three things mentioned before and faith is designated strong and effectual by it. Steadfastness argues a well-grounded, firm, and unshaken assent to the truth of the promises and is therefore opposed to wavering (James 1:5–6). It argues a resolved, clear consent to receive and close with Christ as offered in the promise for life and so it is opposed to doubting. That is troublesome, disquieting, and perplexing doubts. It argues the settled acquiescence of the soul in the choice made and the close consented unto and so it is opposed to abiding trouble (John 14:1).

This steadfastness in believing does not exclude all temptations from without. When we say a tree is firmly rooted, we do not mean that the wind never blows upon it. The house that is built on the rock is not free from assaults and storms. The Captain of our salvation, the author and perfector of our faith was tempted, and we will be too if we follow him. Nor does it exclude all doubting from within. So long as we have flesh, though faith be steadfast, we will have unbelief and that bitter root will bring forth some fruit, more or less according as Satan gets advantage to water it. But it excludes a falling under temptation and consequently that trouble and distress which ensues thereon. As likewise abiding perplexing doubts, which make us stagger to and fro between hope and fear questioning whether we close with Christ or not, whether we have any interest in the promise or not and is attended with disconsolation and dejectedness of spirit with real uncertainty of the event.

This then is that which I intend by steadfastness in believing. The establishment of our hearts in the receiving of Christ as offered by the love of the Father to the peace and settlement of our souls and consciences. That our hearts should be so fixed, settled, and established that we should live in the sense and power of it is exceeding acceptable unto God. There is a twofold evil and mistake among us in the great foundation business of closing with Christ in the promise. Some spend all their days in much darkness and disconsolateness. Disputing it to and fro in their own thoughts whether their portion and interest lie therein or not. They are off and on, living and dying, hoping and fearing, and commonly fear most when they have the best hold, for that is the nature of doubting. When they are quite cast down then they set themselves at work to get up and when they are up to any comfortable persuasion, they instantly fear that all is not well and right.

It is not with them as it should be and so they stagger to and fro all their lives, to the grief of the Spirit of God and the discomfort of their own souls. Others, beginning a serious closing with Christ upon abiding grounds and finding it a work of difficulty and tediousness to flesh and blood relapse into generals and inquire no more but take it for granted that as much is done as they can accomplish and so grow formal and secure. To close both of these evils I will confirm the proposition laid down but before I proceed to that, I will draw some corollaries that arise from what has been spoken in the explication of the proposition already insisted on.

Though a little and weak faith where steadfastness is lacking will carry a man to Christ in heaven, yet it will never carry him there comfortably nor pleasantly. He who only has a weak faith will be put to many desperate plunges. Every blast of temptation will cast him down from his consolation if not turn him aside from his obedience. At best he is like a man bound in a chain on the top of a high tower. Though he cannot fall yet he cannot help but fear. However, it will have a good end.

The least true faith will do its work safely though not so sweetly. True faith in the least degree gives the soul a share in the first resurrection. It is of the vital principle which we receive when we are quickened. Now, be it ever so weak a life we have, yet, it is a life that will never fail because it is of the seed of God which abides. It is incorruptible seed that does not die. A believer is spirit and is quickened from the dead. Be he ever so young, ever so sick, and ever so weak he is still alive, and the second death will have no power over him. A little faith gives a whole Christ. He that has the least faith has as true an interest, though not so clear an interest, in the righteousness of Christ as the most steadfast believer. Others may be more holy than he but not one in the world is more righteous than he. For he is righteous with the righteousness of Christ. He cannot help but be low in sanctification, for a little faith will bring but little or low obedience. If the root be weak, the fruit will not be great. However, he is beneath none in justification. The most imperfect faith will give present justification because it interests the soul in a present Christ. The lowest degree of true faith gives the highest completeness of righteousness (Col. 2:10). You who have but a weak faith have yet a strong Christ, so that though all the world should set itself against your little faith it should not prevail. Sin cannot do it, Satan cannot do it, and hell cannot do it. Though you take but a weak and faint hold on Christ, he takes a sure, strong, and unconquerable hold on you. Have you not often wondered that this spark of heavenly fire should be kept alive in the midst of the sea? It is everlasting. A spark that cannot be quenched. A drop of that fountain that can never be wholly dried up. Jesus Christ takes special care of them that are weak in faith (Isa. 40:11). On whatsoever account they are sick, weak, and unable this good Shepherd takes care of them. He shall rule and they shall abide (Mic. 5:4).

There may be faith, a little faith, where there lacks steadfastness and where there is much doubting. Steadfastness is an eminent qualification that all do not attain to. So that there may be faith where there is doubting, although I do not say there must be. Doubtings in themselves are opposite to believing. They are, if I may so say, unbelieving. A man can hardly believe all his days and never doubt but a man may doubt all his days and never believe. If I see a field overgrown with thistles and weeds, I can say, there may be corn there but the thistles and weeds are not corn. I speak this because some have no better bottom for their quiet than that they have doubted. Doubting may be where faith is, but we cannot conclude that where there is doubting there is faith. For it may rise against presumption and security as well as against believing.

Observe that there is a twofold doubting. One kind of doubt is concerned about the end. Men question what will become of them in the end. They fluctuate about what will be their latter end. Did Balaam not do so when he cried, "Let me die the death of the upright, and let my end be like his" (Num. 23:10)? That wretched man was tossed up and down between hopes and fears. This is common to the vilest person in the world. It is but the shaking of their security if they be alone.

The second kind of doubt is concerned about the means. The soul doubts whether it loves Christ and whether Christ loves it or not. This is far more genuine than the former. It discovers, at least, that such a soul is convinced of the excellency and usefulness of Christ and that it has a valuation for him. It is possible that perhaps this may be jealousy from fervency of love sometimes and not always from weakness of faith. However, with these doubtings, faith, at least a little faith may consist. So, it was with the poor man who cried out, "I believe; help my unbelief" (Mark 9:24). There is believing and unbelieving, faith and doubting, both at work at the same time in the same person. Like Jacob and Esau struggling in the same womb.

Therefore, do not conclude believing from doubting. He that satisfies himself that his field has corn because it has thistles may come short of a harvest. If your fears are more about the end than the means, more about future happiness than present communion with God you can scarce have a clearer argument of a false and corrupt frame of heart. Some flatter themselves that they have doubted and trembled but now they thank God that they are quiet and at rest. They cannot tell how they came to be so. Only where they were disquieted and troubled, now all is well with them. How many of this sort have I known, who, while convictions have been warm upon them, while they have had many perplexing thoughts about their state and condition, after a while their convictions have worn off. Their doubtings which arose from there have departed and they have sunk down into a cold and lifeless frame! This is a miserable bottom of quiet. If there were no way of casting out doubts and fears except by believing then this would be somewhat useful, but presumption and security will do it also, at least for a season. But these things fall in only in reference to what was spoken before. I proceed now to confirm the proposition laid down, according to the explanation given of it before and I will do this first from Scripture testimonies.

How Faith Glorifies God

"He grew strong in his faith as he gave glory to God" (Rom. 4:20). All that God requires of any of the sons of men is his glory, which he will not give unto another (Isaiah 42:8). Let God have his glory and we may take freely whatever we will. Take Christ, take grace, take heaven, and take all. The great glory which he will give to us consists in giving him his glory and beholding of it. Now, if this be the great thing, the only thing that God requires at our hands, and if all which he has reserved to himself is that he be glorified as God, as our God, then he that gives him that gives him what is acceptable to him.

Therefore, Abraham pleased God by being strong or steadfast in believing. He was strong in faith and gave glory to God. The glory of God is spoken of in various senses in the Scripture. One way is the Hebrew word that signifies "weight." The apostle alludes to this when he speaks of, "An eternal weight of glory" (2 Cor. 4:17). This is the glory of the thing itself. It likewise signifies splendor or brightness, where the apostle in like manner speaks of, "The radiance of the glory of God" (Heb. 1:3). Which is the greatness and excellency of beauty in all perfections. In this sense, the infinite excellency of God in his inconceivable perfections raised up in such brightness as utterly exceeds all our apprehensions is called his glory. And so, he is, "The God of glory" (Acts 7:2), or the most glorious God and our Savior is called, "The Lord of glory" in the same sense (1 Cor. 2:8). In this respect we can give no glory to God. We can add nothing to his excellencies nor the infinite, inconceivable brightness of them by anything we do.

Glory relates not only to the thing itself that is glorious but to the estimation and opinion we have of it. That is when that which is in itself glorious is esteemed so and in this respect that which is infinitely glorious in itself may be more or less glorious in its manifestation and the estimation of it. So, glory is not any of God's excellencies or perfections, but it is the esteem and manifestation of them among and unto others. This God declares to be his glory (Exodus 33:19). Moses desires to see the "glory" of God (Ex. 33:18). This God calls his "face" (Ex. 33:20). That is the glory of God in itself, "But" God says, "you cannot see my face" (Ex. 33:20). You cannot see my face which is the brightness of my essential glory or the splendor of my excellencies and perfections.

Well, what then? Will he have no acquaintance with it? After this, God places him in a rock and tells him that he will show him his glory there and this he does under the

FAITH

name of his "back" (Ex. 33:23). That is, he will declare to him wherein and how his glory is manifested. Now, this Rock that followed them was Christ (1 Cor. 10:4). The Lord places Moses in that rock to show him his glory, intimating that there is no glimpse of it to be obtained but only by them who are placed in Christ Jesus. Now, what is this glory of God which he showed to Moses? That he declares causing his majesty or some visible signs of his presence to pass before him (Ex. 34:6). He proclaims the name of God with many gracious properties of his nature and blessedness. As if he should say, "Moses, would you see my glory? This is it. That I may be known to be, 'The Lord, the Lord, a God merciful and gracious' (Ex. 34:6). Let me be known to be this and that is the glory I aim at from the sons of men."

See now how steadfastness in believing gives glory to God. It advances and magnifies all these properties of God and gives all his attributes their due exaltation. An excellent estimation of them is included in it. Might I here descend to particulars I could manifest that there is not any property of God whereby he has made himself known to us but steadfastness in believing gives it the glory which in some measure is due unto it and also that all doubting arises from our calling some divine attribute into question. It was easy to show how this gives God the glory of his faithfulness, truth, power, righteousness, grace, mercy, goodness, love, patience, and whatever else God has revealed himself to be. This then is the force of this first testimony. If the glory of God be all that he requires at our hands and this steadfastness in believing gives him this glory and this alone does so it must needs be acceptable unto him.

A testimony of the same importance is, "The heirs of the promise" (Heb. 6:17–18). Those to whom the great promise of Christ is made are believers. These are said here to, "Have fled for refuge" (Heb. 6:18). These are the fliers with speed. The expression is evidently metaphorical. The allusion, some say, is taken from those who ran in a race for a prize. This, they say, the word that follows (which signifies "to take fast hold on"), does import. Men that run in a race when they attain the end seize on and lay fast hold of the prize. By rendering the word, "Fled for refuge," our translators manifest that they had respect to the manslayers flying to the city of refuge under the Old Testament. Various interpreters go this way, and I am inclined to this acceptance of the metaphor upon a double account.

First, because I think the apostle would more willingly allude to a Hebrew custom writing to the Hebrews touching an institution of God directly typical of the matter he had in hand than to a custom of the Greeks and Romans in their races which had not so much light in it as to the business in hand as the other. Second, because the design of the place does evidently hold out a flying from something

FAITH

as well as a flying to something. In which regard it is said that there is, "Strong encouragement" (Heb. 6:18) provided for them. Namely, in their deliverance from the evil which they feared and fled from. Now, in a race there is indeed a prize proposed but there is no evil avoided. It was otherwise with him that fled for refuge. For as he had a city of safety before him so he had the avenger of blood behind him, and he fled with speed and diligence to the one that he might avoid the other. Now, these cities of refuge were provided for the manslayer, who having slain a man unawares and being surprised with an apprehension of danger because it was lawful for the avenger of blood to slay him, fled with all his strength to one of those cities where he was to enjoy immunity and safety. So, a poor sinner finding himself in a condition of guilt, surprised with a sense of it, seeing death and destruction ready to seize upon him, flies with all his strength to the bosom of the Lord Jesus, the only city of refuge from the avenging justice of God and curse of the law. Now, this flying to the bosom of Christ, the hope set before us for relief and safety is believing. It is here called fleeing by the Holy Ghost to express the nature of it to the spiritual sense of believers. Now, what does he declare himself to be affected with their, "Fleeing for refuge," that is, their believing? Why, he has taken all means possible to show himself abundantly willing to receive them. He has engaged his word and promise that they may not in the least doubt or waver but know that he is ready to receive them and give them, "Strong encouragement" (Ex. 6:18).

What is this encouragement? Where may it appear to arise? When did consolation arise to him who having slain a man unawares should fly to a city of refuge? Must it not be from here? From the gates of the city being certainly open to him so that he could find protection there and be safe guarded from the revenger? Where then must our strong consolation and encouragement be if we thus fly for refuge by believing? Must it not be from here? That God is freely ready to receive us, that he will in no wise shut us out, but that we will be welcome to him and with the more speed we come the more welcome we will be. He convinces us of this by the engagement of his word and oath to that purpose.

What further testimony would we have that our believing is acceptable to him? It is said, "My righteous one shall live by faith, and if he shrinks back, my soul has no pleasure in him" (Heb. 10:38). If any man shrinks back my soul [the Lord's] has no pleasure in him. What is it to draw back? It is to decline from steadfastness of believing. So, the apostle interprets it, "But we are not of those who shrink back and are destroyed, but of those who have faith" (Heb. 10:39). Drawing back is opposed to believing. In those who draw back, that do not come up to steadfastness in believing, nor labor to do so, the Lord's soul has no pleasure. That is, he exceedingly abhors and abominates them. That is the force of that expression. His delight is in those who are steadfast in adhering to the promises and in them his soul takes pleasure.

When the Jews discussed with our Savior about salvation, they asked him, "What must we do, to be doing the works of God" (John 6:28)? That work of God by which they might come to be accepted with him, which is the cry of all convinced persons. Our Savior's answer is, "This is the work of God, that you believe in him whom he has sent" (John 6:29). Will you know the great work wherein God is so delighted? It is this, he says, that you believe and be steadfast therein. There are also many exhortations that are given us by the Holy Ghost to come up unto steadfastness (Heb. 12:12; Isa. 35), but I will not farther insist on testimonies which exceedingly abound to this purpose.

The next will consist in the further improvement of the first testimony concerning the glory of God arising from our being steadfast in believing. This is granted by all, that God's ultimate end in all things he does himself, and in all that he requires us to do is his own glory. It cannot be otherwise if he be the first and only independent being, the prime cause of all things, and their chief good. God having placed his glory in that which cannot be attained and brought about without believing, in answer to his present constitution of things, it must needs be acceptable to him as is a suitable means to a designed end to anyone's acting in wisdom and righteousness. Bear in mind what it is that I mean by believing. Though the word be general and large yet in my intendment it is restrained to the particulars insisted on. Namely, the constant establishment of our souls in receiving the Lord Jesus offered unto us in the truth and from the love of the Father for the pardon of sins and acceptance of our persons before God. This, I say, according to God's constitution of things in the covenant of grace is necessary to bring about that end of glory to himself which he aims at.

Therefore, he sums up his whole design to be, "The praise of his glorious grace" (Eph. 1:6). In Proverbs 25:2 this is clearly asserted, "It is the glory of God to conceal things," or to cover a matter. I told you before what the glory of God is. It is not the splendor and majesty of his infinite and excellent perfections which do not arise from anything he does but from what he is. It is the exaltation, manifestation, and essence of those excellencies. When God is received, believed, and known to be such as he declares himself to be, therein is he glorified. That is his glory. The Holy Ghost says this glory arises from the covering a matter. What matter is this? It is not the glory of God to cover every matter or all things whatsoever. Yea, it is his glory to, "Bring to light things now hidden in the darkness" (1 Cor. 4:5). The manifestation of his own works declares his glory (Psalm 19:1). So also the manifestation of the good works of his people (Matt. 5:16). These things hidden are of some peculiar kind. The following opposition discovers this, "The glory of kings is to search things out" (Prov. 25:2). What matter is it that is the glory of the king to find out? Is it not faults and offenses against the law? Is it not the glory of magistrates to find out transgressions so that the transgressors may be punished? The glory of the magistrate is to inquire, find out, and punish offenses and transgressions of the law. It is then in answer here unto a sinful thing, sin itself, that is the matter or thing which it is the glory of God to cover.

But what is it to cover a sinful matter? It is that which is opposed to the magistrate's finding it out. We have a full description of what that is in Job 29:16–17: "I searched out the cause of him whom I did not know. I broke the fangs of the unrighteous." It is to make judicial inquisition after, to find out hidden transgressions so that the offenders may be brought to deserved punishment. So, God's concealing a matter is his not searching with an intention of punishment into sins and sinners in order to make them naked to the stroke of the law. It is his hiding of sin from the condemning power of the law. The word used here is the same as that of David in Psalm 32:1, "Blessed is the one whose transgression is forgiven; whose sin is covered." In various other places it is used to the same purpose which is expressed by another as, "You will cast all our sins into the depths of the sea" (Micah 7:19). That which is so disposed of is utterly covered from the sight of men. So, God expresses the covering of the sins of his people as their not appearing to their condemnation. They will be cast into the depths of the sea.

Hence in the New Testament all our sins are said to be forgiven. The word signifies properly to remove or dismiss one. It means to send away or remove our sins out of sight. The same in substance with that which is here said, "To cover." And so is the word used in another business, "You have neglected the weightier matters of the law" (Matt. 23:23). That is, you have laid them aside, as it were, out of sight and are taking no thought of them. Now, the bottom of all these expressions of removing, hiding, covering, and concealing sin which gives life and significance to them, making them import forgiveness of sin is the allusion that is in them to the mercy-seat under the law. The making and the use of it we have in Exodus 25:17–18. It was a plate of pure gold lying on the ark called a covering. In the ark written on tables of stone was the law. Over the mercy seat, between the cherubim was the oracle representing the presence of God. By which the Holy Ghost does signify that the mercy-seat was to cover the law and the condemning power of it, as it were, from the eye of God's justice that we be not consumed.

Therefore, is God said to cover sin because by the mercy-seat he hides that which is the strength and power of sin as to its guilt and tendency unto punishment. The apostle calls this, "Mercy-seat" (Heb 9:5). That word is used only once more in the New Testament, and it is in reference to

FAITH

Christ. Whom God has put forward as a mercy seat (Rom. 3:25). Christ alone is that mercy seat by whom sin and the law from where sin has its rigor is hidden. And from that typical institution is that expression in the Old Testament, "Hide me in the shadow of your wings" (Ps. 17:8). The wings of the cherubim where the mercy seat was, that is, in the bosom of Christ. Now, the Holy Ghost says, to hide, to cover, and to pardon sin by Christ is the glory of God wherein he will be exalted and admired and for which he will be praised. Give him this and you give him his great aim and design. Let him be believed in and trusted on as God in Christ pardoning iniquity, transgression, and sin, and so reconciling the world to himself and manifesting his glorious properties therein and he has his end.

Should I now proceed to show what God has done, what he does, and will do to set up his glory it would make it evident, indeed, that he aimed at it. His eternal electing love lies at the bottom of this design. The tendency of it is that God may be glorified in the forgiveness of sin. The sending of his Son which is a mystery of wisdom, goodness, and righteousness past finding out. With all that by his authority and commission he did, suffered, and does was that his name might be glorified in this thing. Has the new covenant of grace any other end? Did God not on purpose propose, make, and establish that covenant in the blood of his Son? That whereas he had by his works of creation and providence by the old covenant and law given glory to himself in other respects he might by this glorify himself in the hiding of iniquity? The dispensation of the Spirit for the conversion of sinners with all the mighty works ensuing there upon is to the same and no other purpose. Wherefore does God exercise patience, forbearance, and long-suffering towards us such as he will be admired for eternity, such as our souls stand amazed to think of? It is only that he may bring about this glory of his. Namely, the covering of iniquity and the pardoning of sin. Now, what is it that is required on our part that this great design of God for his glory may be accomplished in and towards us? Is it not our believing and steadfastness therein? I need not stay to manifest it nor yet give farther light or strength to our inference from what has been spoken. I mean that if these things are so then our believing and steadfastness therein are exceedingly acceptable to God.

For the last demonstration of the point I will add the consideration of one particular that God uses in the pursuit of his glory that is mentioned before and that is his institution and command of preaching the gospel to all nations and the great care he has taken to provide instruments for the propagation of it and proclamation therein of the word of his grace. "Go into all the world and proclaim the gospel to the whole creation" (Mark 16:15). "Go therefore and make disciples of all nations" (Matt. 28:19). What is this gospel which he will have preached and declared? Is it anything but a declaration of his mind and will concerning his gracious acceptance of believing and steadfastness therein? This God declares of his purpose and his eternal, unchangeable will. That there is by his appointment an infallible, inviolable connection between believing on Jesus Christ, the receiving of him, and the everlasting enjoyment of himself. This he declares to all but his purpose to bestow faith effectually relates only to some, "As many as were appointed to eternal life believed" (Acts 13:48). But this purpose of his will, that believing in Christ will have the end mentioned, righteousness and salvation in the enjoyment of himself concerns all alike.

TWO

*The Use of Faith in a Time
of Public Calamity*

"The righteous shall live by his faith" (Hab. 2:4). This is the first time these words are mentioned in the Scripture but three times they are quoted by the apostle Paul. He preached, as it were, three times upon them (Rom. 1:17; Gal. 3:11; Heb. 10:38). For it is full of heavenly matter and is made use of by the apostle for several purposes. I do not know of one text that has been preached upon more or written upon more by those who have treated the life of faith than this one. How the just live the life of justification and how they live the life of sanctification. The life of consolation, the life of peace, the life of joy, the life of obedience, etc. My design is of quite another nature and is that which falls in with the design of the prophet in the

FAITH

first use of the words as we will presently see.

You know that for many years upon all these occasions without failing I have been warning you continually of an approaching calamitous time and considering the sins that have been the causes of it. The day is with the Lord. I do not know the year and month, but I have told you that judgment will begin at the household of God (1 Pet. 4:17), that in the latter days of the church perilous times will come (2 Tim. 3:1), that God seems to have hardened our hearts from his fear and caused us to err from his ways (Isa. 63:17), and that none knows what the power of his wrath will be. In all these things I have foretold you of perilous, distressing, calamitous times and in all men's apprehensions they now lie at the door and are entering in upon us. Now I must change my design and my present work will be both upon this and to show how we ought to behave ourselves in and under the approaches of distressing calamities that are coming upon us and may reach up to the very neck.

What this text teaches us is that in the approaches of overwhelming calamities and in the view of them we ought to live by faith in a peculiar manner. That is the meaning of the place and that this is our duty appears from this passage and the context. For the prophet had received a vision, a dreadful vision from God of the Chaldeans coming in, and of the destruction they would bring upon the church and upon all the land (Hab. 1). Having received this vision he considers what his own duty is and what the duty of the church is in the approaches of this distressing, calamitous season. Why, he says, "I will take my stand at my watchpost and station myself on the tower, and look out to see what he will say to me, and what I will answer concerning my complaint" (Hab. 2:1). It is as though the prophet is saying, God will reprove me and there will be great arguing between God and my soul. I know my own guilt and sin and I would be in a readiness to have something to answer God when I am reproved and something to commit myself unto. And the answer that he says he will commit himself unto is this, "The righteous shall live by his faith" (Hab. 2:4).

Two things are included here. First, he says, "I will commit myself" (as the apostle makes use of it), "Unto Jesus Christ for righteousness. I have nothing else to answer God when I am reproved." Second, he says, "I will pass through all these terrible and dreadful dispensations of providence that are coming upon me by living the life of faith." A peculiar way of living as we will presently see.

When the flood was coming upon the world Noah was, "A herald of righteousness" (2 Pet. 2:5). What righteousness did Noah preach? Why, that righteousness whereof he himself was partaker. For he, "Became an heir of the righteousness that comes by faith" (Heb. 11:7). When the flood was coming Noah preached the righteousness of faith to the world so that they might escape if they would

FAITH

attend unto it. But it was rejected by them. Wherefore, in the approach of a calamitous season there is in a special way and manner of living by faith required of us. But you will say, "What is a calamitous season?" or "When do you consider a season calamitous?" I will give you two things for the description of such a season as I judge to be manifestly calamitous.

When it exceeds the bounds of affliction or when the dispensations of God's anger in it cannot be reduced to the head of affliction. "Son of man, prophesy and say, thus says the Lord, say: 'A sword, a sword is sharpened and also polished, sharpened for slaughter, polished to flash like lightning! (Or shall we rejoice? You have despised the rod, my son, with everything of wood). For it will not be a testing—what could it do if you despise the rod?' declares the Lord God" (Ezek. 21:9–10, 13). Now, I say, let it be what it will, when a calamity comes upon a people or the church of God that cannot be reduced to the head of affliction but that everyone will find there is anger, judgment, and wrath in it then it is a distressing time.

When judgments fall promiscuously upon all sorts of persons and make no distinction then I take it to be a distressing time. For they strip men of the comforts they cherish in their own minds. "It is all one; therefore, I say, 'He destroys both the blameless and the wicked.' When disaster brings sudden death, he mocks at the calamity of the innocent" (Job 9:22–23). When God brings a scourge or a sword that will slay indiscriminately, that will seize upon, destroy, and devour the innocent so that they will not escape, he will be as one that stands by rejoicing to see how they carry themselves under their trial.

Now, this is enough to give satisfaction as to what I mean by a distressing, calamitous time. It cannot be reduced to the head of affliction, and it slays suddenly and promiscuously the perfect and the wicked. It may be that the good figs shall go first into captivity (Jer. 24). I am not much otherwise minded, and God may have mercy for them in that dispensation. I will now show you these two things: 1. How we shall live by faith. How we should behave ourselves. What faith will do in such a season. What our duty is under the approach of these calamitous, distressing times that are coming upon us. 2. I will show you how faith does and will carry itself under other perplexities that we have upon us that we either feel or fear.

What Faith Does in Distress
First, what our duty is under the approach of these distressing, calamitous times that are coming upon us and what faith will do in such a season. Faith will guide and move the soul under the approach of these distressing calamities in these following things.

Faith Fears God
Faith will give the soul a reverential fear of God in his

FAITH

judgments. So, it did unto the saints of old: "By faith Noah, being warned by God concerning events as yet unseen, in reverent fear constructed an ark for the saving of his household" (Heb. 11:7). There is no man that is not stout-hearted and far from righteousness, but is, upon God's warning moved with a reverential fear of God in his judgments. It was so with David, "My flesh trembles for fear of you, and I am afraid of your judgments" (Ps. 119:120). He was not afraid as to outward judgments but under them his flesh trembled with a reverential fear of God. And so it was with the prophet Habakkuk upon the vision he had of the approach of the Chaldeans, "I hear, and my body trembles; my lips quiver at the sound; rottenness enters into my bones; my legs tremble beneath me. Yet I will quietly wait for the day of trouble to come upon people who invade us" (Hab. 3:16). He had a reverential fear of God in his judgments working upon him. According to my best observation of things in this state wherein we are, the generality of people may be distributed under these three heads.

There are some that are, indeed, afraid of approaching judgments. They do not know how soon they will reach unto themselves, their persons, their families, their relations, their estates, etc. All that they have labored for and exerted their utmost care and industry about in the world, the flood flies at the door, ready to carry all before it. They fear every day. Some men die by the fear of dying. They are poor for fear of poverty. They will part with nothing because they fear they must part with all. A strange contradiction of spirit! Now this is not the work of faith. So far as it prevails upon any of our spirits, God will rebuke us for it. He declares, "I, I am he who comforts you; who are you that you are afraid of man who dies, of the son of man who is made like grass, and have forgotten the Lord, your Maker, who stretched out the heavens and laid the foundations of the earth, and you fear continually all the day because of the wrath of the oppressor, when he sets himself to destroy? And where is the wrath of the oppressor" (Isa. 51:12–13)? And have you not sanctified the Lord in thy heart nor made him your fear (Isa. 8:13)? Who are you? God hates this sinful fear. It is an abomination unto him. This is nothing but the fear of self. We will keep all warm about us while we are in this world and are afraid of the broom of destruction.

There are others who utterly despise these things and take no notice of them. Those who do not think any such distressing calamity will come upon them. If it does, they will deal well enough with it. "Therefore, hear the word of the Lord, you scoffers, who rule this people in Jerusalem! Because you have said, "We have made a covenant with death, and with Sheol we have an agreement, when the overwhelming whip passes through it will not come to us" (Isa. 28:14–15). They have a thousand ways to disinterest themselves from anything of the most distressing calamity that is coming over the world. This swallows up most of mankind and is that which the prophet does so reflect upon: "O Lord, your hand is lifted up, but they do not see it. Let them see your zeal for your people and be ashamed. Let the fire for your adversaries consume them" (Isa. 26:11).

The other sort is mentioned in Judges 5:6 and may be called way-side men. Idle men that have nothing else to do but to walk up and down and talk and are not concerned with a reverence of God and his judgments. They talk of them as if there were no God in heaven to regard them or as if they had no concern with him. If we have the least, true and saving faith in exercise it will cast this cursed frame out of our hearts. It will be daily working it out of our souls and will bring us to that which I told you is its proper work. God, says the psalmist, "has made himself known; he has executed judgment" (Ps. 9:16). And what of God is principally known in the judgments which he executes in the world is considered but a little. That which God makes known of himself in a peculiar manner in these dreadful dispensations is his majesty, his holiness, and his power.

God will appear to be awfully majestic and wonderfully glorious in such dispensations. He speaks of himself upon that occasion, "In that day mankind will cast away their idols of silver and their idols of gold, which they made for themselves to worship, to the moles and to the bats, to enter the caverns of the rocks and the clefts of the cliffs, from before the terror of the Lord, and from the splendor of his majesty, when he rises to terrify the earth" (Isa. 2:20–21). If we have the light of faith to let it in then we will see a majesty and glory in God's actions, even in his public and distressing judgments. Such a greatness and a glory that the soul will be constrained to bow down before him.

God does in his judgments also manifest his holiness of which we will speak afterward. We will say, "Who will not fear, O Lord, and glorify your name? For you alone are holy. All nations will come and worship you, for your righteous acts have been revealed" (Rev. 15:4). When God makes manifest his judgments his holiness will appear. So, when Habakkuk came to plead with God about that great judgment of the Chaldeans he cries out, "O Lord my God, my Holy One, you who are of purer eyes than to see evil and cannot look at wrong" (Hab. 1:12–13). In them God also glorifies himself in his power. He sets up one and pulls down another and does whatsoever he pleases. Herein he manifestly shows his sovereign power.

Now, to live by faith is to cast out all those cursed frames mentioned before and to bring this frame into your hearts as the foundation of all that follows. Namely, that you have a reverential fear of the majesty, holiness, and power of God in all his judgments and without this we will not please God in anything we do. These are the true sayings of God. If there be another frame in us this dispensation will pierce to the very soul before it be over.

FAITH

Faith Prepares an Ark

Where faith has filled the soul with a reverential fear of God its first work will be to put the soul upon preparing and providing an ark for itself. So, it was in the great example of our faith mentioned before. Noah, "In reverent fear constructed an ark for the saving of his household" (Heb. 11:7). Let men pretend what they will but unless they are under a strange and careless stupidity and security (which, I fear, is upon most professors), they cannot in such a season as this keep from preparing some reserve for themselves. What will we do when this comes upon us? They have some prevalent reserve: "A rich man's wealth is his strong city" (Prov. 18:11). He may lose a great deal, but he will save enough for himself. So, the strong man trusts to his strength and the wise man to his wisdom. Men prepare one thing or other for themselves to be an ark against the coming storm and those who do not so fluctuate up and down at uncertainties hoping that by one way or another, that they know not of, they will be carried above all. That it will not be as this or that prophet or minister says but that by some way they will escape. This is to not prepare an ark, which is the work of faith to do. Here I will inquire into two things: 1. What is this ark that is to be prepared? 2. How we ought to enter it or how we are to make especial entrance into it in reference to an approaching calamitous season.

What is this ark that is to be prepared? This ark is Jesus

Christ and faith in him is necessary. In this chapter of my text where inquiry is made what will be answered unto God and what course will be taken upon the coming flood of the Chaldeans, this is the course to be taken, "The righteous shall live by his faith" (Hab. 2:4). What is that? It is to seek for righteousness by Christ. To seek afresh for justification and life by Christ. There is no other way and no other ark. He is described as this ark in that well known place, "And a man (that is, Jesus Christ) shall be as an hiding-place from the wind, and a covert from the tempest, as rivers of water in a dry place, as the shadow of a great rock in a weary land" (Isa. 32:2, KJV). That is the ark and I do not know how to better describe what I mean by securing ourselves in the ark than like the description the prophet gives here, though in metaphorical terms. Likewise, in Micah 5:5, having given a promise of Christ, he adds, "And he shall be their peace. When the Assyrian comes into our land."

To take ourselves to the ark is to take ourselves to the fountain of our peace. How then do we receive this peace if God's wrath be kindled but a little? The psalmist says, "Blessed are all who (commit themselves unto him) take refuge in him" (Ps. 2:12). In whom? In the Son. For he says, "Kiss the Son" (Ps. 2:12). And surely my brethren the wrath of God is now kindled, not a little, but a great deal in all sorts and ways. The indications of the wrath of God are upon the spirits of men of all sorts. Of professors

FAITH

and of the world, in their own persons, in all societies and relations. Where are we then to take ourselves but unto Christ? "Blessed are all who take refuge in him" (Ps. 2:12).

But now it would not have benefited either Noah or his sons to have an ark prepared for them unless they had a door to the ark. God, in effect, told them to build a door so that they may have entrance. To obtain an interest in Christ is the general work of faith all our days. But how will we be able now to make a special entrance into this ark suitable unto the state and condition in which we are and to approach a calamitous season that is hastening upon us? I know but of one way for our making a special entrance into this ark, Jesus Christ, in reference to such a season, which is, the solemn renovation of our covenant with God. This is the way that has been used by the church from the foundation of the world without any instance of the contrary. When a storm was coming, if ever they were delivered from it, they entered the ark by the renovation of their covenant with God. And seeing the end is certain we are to enter afresh into this ark, Jesus Christ. It is no wisdom in civil things to remove a means unless we have a better to substitute in the place of it and it is so in spirituals.

I desire all that fear God to stir up their hearts and thoughts and offer to us (if they can) a better way for this church or any church to enter the ark in the approach of a storm than this and it will be embraced. This church has done so, though I begin to fear some look upon it as a very dead, sluggish commodity they know not how to trade with. But do not be mistaken, no such thing lies by you in the sight of God this day. Do not despond, the day is approaching when others shall come and, "Shall take hold of the robe of a Jew, saying, 'Let us go with you, for we have heard that God is with you'" (Zech. 8:23). Some have gone further than us already in zeal, warmth, and courage under a sense of engagements that are upon them. Blessed be God and let his holy name be exalted! I look for no safety and no deliverance in the trials and afflictions that are coming upon the earth but what is had in the way of believing. I value not those that are otherwise minded. Bless God who has provided for you this door of entrance before the flood comes and the rain falls. Bless God for it, make use of it, and be able to plead it with God. Let the Lord know that you have made your choice to be his and are under his care and not under the protection of the world. I will not say you will be saved temporally, but you shall be saved eternally. I cannot say that you will have peace with men, but you shall have peace with God. I cannot say that you will not lose your lives, but I will say that you shall not lose your souls.

Our principal concern is for you to make good your entrance. A door made into the ark will do you no good unless you enter in and make good your entrance at the door. How will we make good our entrance into the ark that we may have safety therein? If we are not at this work, we have no faith. Stand to your engagements and stand to the performance of those duties God requires at your hands. Not only as there is no one thing required but what is a special duty of the new covenant but stand to them now as those that have been your entrance into the ark where God will give you all that rest that you can be partakers of in this world. This is another work of faith in the approach of a calamitous time.

Faith Searches the Heart

If we live by faith in the approach of a calamitous season this will put us upon the search and examination of our own hearts. To determine what accession that we have made to the sins that have procured these judgments. This is that which faith (where it is in any measure sincere) will assuredly put us upon and it is that God does now in an especial manner call for. Now, the sins which do and have procured these judgments are of two sorts: 1. The open and scandalous sins of the world, and 2. The sins of churches and professors.

The open and scandalous sins of the world. The apostle reckons them up together: "Do not be deceived: neither the sexually immoral, nor idolaters, nor adulterers, nor men who practice homosexuality, nor thieves, nor the greedy, nor drunkards, nor revilers, nor swindlers will inherit the kingdom of God" (1 Cor. 6:9–10). He does it again in Ephesians 5:5–6, "For you may be sure of this, that everyone who is sexually immoral or impure, or who is covetous (that is, an idolater), has no inheritance in the kingdom of Christ and God. Let no one deceive you with empty words, for because of these things the wrath of God comes upon the sons of disobedience." He reckons them up also in Galatians 5:19–21, "Now the works of the flesh are evident: sexual immorality, impurity, sensuality, idolatry, sorcery, enmity, strife, jealousy, fits of anger, rivalries, dissensions, divisions, envy, drunkenness, orgies, and things like these. I warn you, as I warned you before, that those who do such things will not inherit the kingdom of God."

Every man may read an exposition of these things in the practice of multitudes. Some will say they bless God that they are free from these things and so they hope they have had no hand in procuring the judgments of God that are coming upon the nation. Let them fall upon them and their interest who are guilty of these provoking abominations. For which the wrath of God is revealed from heaven against their ungodliness. Why, it is well if they are not guilty of any of these sins but the seed and foundation, even of all these sins, lie in our nature if not in our persons and what eruptions they have made towards the provoking the eyes of God's glory I know not. But suppose you have escaped these pollutions that are in the world through lust there are other sins.

FAITH

There are the sins of churches and of professors that in reference to Christ's mediatory kingdom have as great influence for the procuring of judgments as the worst sins of the world have for the procuring of judgments in his providential kingdom. I know a time when there was a storm wherein a whole vessel and all that were in it were like to have been cast away but there was only one in the ship that was the cause of the storm—Jonah.

I will just mention the judgment-procuring sins of churches and professors which are reduced in Scripture to these four heads. First, lukewarmness, which was the judgment-procuring sin of Laodicea. Second, contenting ourselves in outward order and freedom from scandal. This was the judgment-procuring sin of Sardis and will prove ruinous to the best churches in the world. Third, a lack of love among ourselves and division in churches. Fourth, earthly mindedness. Love of the world and conformity to it that is found among the generality of professors.

THREE

*The Use of Faith Under
Reproaches and Persecutions*

"Clouds and thick darkness are all around him; righteousness and justice are the foundation of his throne" (Ps. 97:2). From here we have taken occasion to consider what is our especial duty when clouds and darkness are round about us as they are at this day. And some of you know I have had a great persuasion that the clouds that are gathering will, at least in their first storm, fall upon the people of God. I must repeat it again and again. I have been warning you for some years and telling you it would be so. The present frame of conflict I have in my own spirit, that frame of spirit which I have observed in others, and the state and condition of all churches and professors, so far as I know, is they are gone into a dreadful security. I

FAITH

speak my heart and what I know with reference unto our present state and the cause of God. We are gone into a dismal security. Which still confirms to me that the storm will come upon us and that it will not be long before we feel it. My design is therefore to show you how we ought to behave ourselves under the perplexities and difficulties that we are to conflict with in this world. I have not sat studying for things to speak but only tell you the experience of my own heart and what I am laboring after. I have already shown you what our duty is under the approach of these distressing, calamitous times that are coming upon us and what faith will do in such a season.

I am now to show in the second place how faith will carry itself under other perplexities that are either present or are coming upon us. Here I will show you first, how we may live by faith under all the reproaches and persecutions that do or may befall us upon the account of that order and fellowship of the gospel and of that way of God's worship which we do profess. Second, how we may live by faith with reference unto the returning upon us of antichristian darkness and cruelty if God will suffer it to be so. Third, how we may live by faith under an apprehension of great and woeful decays in churches, in church members, in professors of all sorts, and in the gradual with-drawings of the glory of God from us upon that account.

How may we live by faith with reference unto those reproaches that scorn and contempt which are cast upon the ways of God which we profess, that worship of God wherein we are engaged, and that order of the gospel that we do observe with the persecutions that will attend us upon the account thereof? Truly, I may say of it as the Jews said to Paul about Christianity, "For with regard to this sect we know that everywhere it is spoken against" (Acts 28:22). The whole world seems to be combined that the name of Israel, in this way, may no more be had in remembrance. There are few that are concerned about these things while it is well with them, their families, their relations, estates, inheritances, etc. Let the ways of God be reproached, what is that to them? They are not concerned in it. They cannot say as the psalmist does when he speaks in the person of Christ, "The reproaches of those who reproach you have fallen on me" (Ps. 69:9). Perhaps some of us are more sensible than others (or, at least, have reason so to be) of those reproaches that are continually cast upon the ways of God seeing they are more particularly upon us. But to those that are not concerned in this scorn and contempt I would say three things.

First, what evidence do you have that you have a concern in God's glory? For these things are those whereby God is glorified in this world and if you are not concerned when there are so many reflections thrown upon it then consider what evidence you have in yourselves of any concern in the glory of God. Second, what evidence have you that you have a love to these things that can hear them reproached, scorned, contemned, and never be moved by it? An honest and good man would find himself concerned if his wife or children were reproached with lies and shameful things because of his interest in them. But for them that can hear the ways of God reproached every day and so long as it is well with them and theirs are not concerned can have no evidence that they have a love unto them. Nehemiah cries out upon such an occasion, "Hear, O our God, for we are despised. Turn back their taunt on their own heads and give them up to be plundered in a land where they are captives" (Neh. 4:4). God has made special promises to such as are concerned, "I will gather those of you who mourn for the festival, so that you will no longer suffer reproach" (Zeph. 3:18). Whom will he gather? Them that are sorrowful for the solemn assembly, who are of thee, to whom the reproach of it was a burden. The solemn assemblies were reproached and mocked and there were some of them (not all) to whom this reproach was a burden. "These," God says, "I will gather under my gracious protection." Third, to add one more word. If you are not concerned in the reproaches that are cast upon the ways of God, then persecution shall awaken you and either make you concerned or put an end unto all your profession.

How Faith Performs under Persecution
Now, the inquiry is how we will glorify God under these

difficulties that we have to face and how we will pass through them without loss unto our spiritual advantage. The apostle, in the tenth chapter to the Hebrews, where he describes this very condition, I have been speaking of fully directs us. "You endured," he says, "a hard struggle with sufferings sometimes being publicly exposed to reproach and affliction, and sometimes being partners with those so treated. For you had compassion on those in prison, and you joyfully accepted the plundering of your property" (Heb. 10:32–34). But how shall we carry ourselves under this condition here described? Now, he says, "The righteous shall live by faith" (Heb. 10:38).

What is the work of faith in this condition that we may glorify God and carry it through to a good and comfortable issue to ourselves? Call your own hearts to an account and see how faith will work to give you support and supply. I will tell you what I am labouring after in my own heart and the Lord direct you to find out what will be more useful! What will faith do in such a case?

Faith will give us such an experience of the power, efficacy, sweetness, and benefit of gospel ordinances and gospel worship as will cause us to despise all that the world can do in opposition unto us. Here I would cast my anchor and exhort you not to be confident of yourselves because nothing else will keep and preserve you. An opinion, a well-grounded opinion and judgment will not preserve you. Love to this or that man's ministry will not preserve

FAITH

you. That you are able to debate for your ways will not preserve you (I can give you instances wherein they have all failed). Resolutions that if all men should leave them, you would not, are insufficient. Nothing can preserve you but a sense and experience of the usefulness and sweetness of gospel administrations according to the mind of Jesus Christ. Faith alone can give you this. The apostle Peter says, "Long for the pure spiritual milk, that by it you may grow up into salvation" (1 Pet. 2:2). Desire and labour to continue in the ordinances of the gospel and the worship of God under the administration of the word. How? "If indeed you have tasted that the Lord is good" (1 Pet. 2:3). Otherwise, you will never desire it. I should hope that through the grace of God (and otherwise I do not hope it), I might yet continue an experience that in the dispensation of the word I find a constant exercise of faith in God, delight in him, and love to him. If I find that I come to the word as expecting to receive from God a sense of his love and supply of his grace I should then have good hope through grace that ten thousand difficulties should never shake me in my continuance in this way. If, however, it be otherwise there will be no continuance nor abiding.

I mention these things because to my best observation, there is a mighty coldness and indifferency grown upon the spirits of men in attending to the worship of God. There is not that life, spirit, courage, and delight in it as there have been in times past. And if so, God only knows where it may end. This I say is the first thing that faith will do in this state if we set it to work. If we would but labour to stir up faith to find those supplies of spiritual life and strength in the ways of his worship and ordinances, if we would labour to overcome prejudices and set ourselves against sloth and negligence, we should find ourselves as other men and greatly set at liberty as to what the world can do unto us. This is that which faith can do for us in such a state of things, and this is what I would be laboring to bring my own heart unto.

Faith in such a season will bring the soul into such an experimental sense of the authority of Jesus Christ as to make it despise all other things. I confess if it were not for the authority of Christ, I would renounce all your meetings. They would have neither form nor comeliness in them why they should be desired. But a deep respect unto the authority of Christ (unless our evil hearts are betrayed by unbelief and weakness) is that which will carry us through all that may befall us. Faith will work this double respect unto the authority of Christ. First, as he is the great head and lawgiver of the church who alone has received all power from the Father to institute all worship and whoever imposes here usurps his crown and dignity. All power to institute spiritual worship is given unto Christ in heaven and in earth. What then? Go therefore, he says, and teach men to observe all that I have commanded you (Matt. 28:18–20). Bring your souls to this exercise of faith

FAITH

so that those things we do are commanded us by Christ who is the sovereign Lord of our consciences and has sovereign authority over our souls. We must all appear before his judgment-seat who will require of us whether we have done and observed what he has commanded us or not. Do not only say these things but labor greatly by faith to affect your consciences with this authority of Christ and you will find that all other authorities will come to nothing however you may suffer for it.

Second, faith respects the authority of Christ as, "Lord of lords, and King of kings" (Rev. 17:14). As he sits at the right hand of God expecting all his enemies to become his footstool (Heb. 10:13). As he has not only a golden sceptre in his hand, "A sceptre of uprightness" (Heb. 1:8), wherewith he rules his church but also an iron rod to break all his enemies in pieces like a potter's vessel. If faith exercises itself upon this power and authority of Christ over his enemies it will pour contempt upon all that the world can do. You cannot be carried before any magistrate, but Christ is there present, greater than them all. Who has their breath in his hands, their lives, and their ways at his disposal, and can do what he pleases with them? Faith will bring in the presence of Christ in such a season when otherwise your hearts would fail for fear and you would be left unto your own wisdom, which is folly, and your own strength, which is but weakness. But if you have faith working in the sense of this authority it will make you like those well-composed persons in the third chapter of Daniel. Do not wonder at the greatness of their answer and the composure of their spirits when they looked on the fiery furnace on the one hand and the fiery countenance of terrible majesty on the other. "If this be so, our God" they said, "whom we serve is able to deliver us from the burning fiery furnace, and he will deliver us out of your hand, O king, but if not, be it known to you, O king, that we will not serve your gods or worship the golden image that you have set up" (Dan. 3:17-18). Faith will give us the same composure of spirit, the same resolution, and with these same things we should relieve ourselves under the worst that can befall us.

Third, faith in such a case and condition will recall and make effectual upon our souls the examples of them that have gone before us in giving the same testimony that we do and in the sufferings that they underwent upon that account. When the apostle had told the believing Hebrews that through all their trials, tribulations, and sufferings they must live by faith they might have asked what encouragement they would receive by faith (Heb. 10). Why, he says, "Faith will bring to mind all the examples of them that have gone before you, that have suffered and been afflicted and distressed as you now are." Which account takes up the whole eleventh chapter of Hebrews and a good part of the beginning of the twelfth. It is a great thing when faith revives an example. Let us then by faith carry in our minds the examples that are recorded in the

FAITH

Scripture.

There is the example of Moses that the apostle gives us, and it is an eminent instance. He writes of Moses, "Choosing rather to be mistreated with the people of God than to enjoy the fleeting pleasures of sin. He considered the reproach of Christ greater wealth than the treasures of Egypt" (Heb. 11:25-26). He endured the reproach of Christ by the dark promise he had to live upon. My brethren take the prophets for an example of them that have suffered and consider how the apostles have gone before us. However, do not stop at them for there is a greater than Moses, and the prophets, and apostles, and even greater than a cloud of witnesses and that is no less a person than the Lord Jesus Christ. "Looking to Jesus, the founder and perfecter of our faith, who for the joy that was set before him endured the cross, despising the shame" (Heb. 12:2). He underwent the contradiction of sinners against himself "and is seated at the right hand of the throne of God" (Heb. 12:2). Faith calling to mind these great examples would give us great support under all the trials we may be brought unto and conflict with. Where are we going? What do we hope for? We would be where Moses is and where the prophets are but how did they get there? They did not get there through the increase of riches and multiplying to themselves lordships in the world but by sufferings and the cross. Through many tribulations they entered the kingdom of heaven.

Fourth, faith will receive in the supplies that Christ has laid up for his people in such a season. Christ has made peculiar provision for suffering saints, and it consists in two things. First, in his special presence with them. He will be with them in the fire and in the water. Second, in the communication of the sense of God's love unto them. "Suffering produces endurance, and endurance produces character, and character produces hope, and hope does not put us to shame, because God's love has been poured into our hearts through the Holy Spirit who has been given to us" (Rom. 5:3–5). Faith will bring all these things into the soul, but your minds must be spiritual, or you cannot exercise one act of faith for bringing in this special provision that is laid up for suffering saints. Very few attain the spiritual frame, where faith fetches in these spiritual consolations Christ hath prepared for such souls. This is one way whereby we may live by faith in such a season. Search therefore and make inquiry in your entrance into troubles what sense faith gives you of the love of God to carry you through these difficulties.

Fifth, it is faith alone that can relieve us with respect unto the recompense of reward. Moses chose "to be mistreated with the people of God; for he was looking to the reward" (Heb. 11:25–26). The light and momentary affliction which we undergo in this world "is preparing for us an eternal weight of glory beyond all comparison" (2 Cor. 4:17). Who knows? In a few days some of us may be taken into that incomprehensible glory where we shall eternally admire that ever we did put any manner of weight on things here below. Faith will fix your eye on the eternal recompense of reward. We have, indeed, a faith now at work that fixes the minds of men upon this and that way of deliverance and this and that strange accident, but we shall find that true faith will burn up all this as stubble.

Sixth, faith will work by patience. The apostle tells us that we "have need of endurance, so that when you have done the will of God you may receive what is promised" (Heb. 10:36). And that we are to be "imitators of those who through faith and patience inherit the promises" (Heb. 6:12). This is something of what I had to offer unto you, and I hope both seasonable and useful. However, it is what I can attain unto in these times of reproach, scorn, and contempt that are cast upon us and are approaching. I say that faith will discover to us that efficacy, sweetness, power, and advantage in spiritual ordinances as to make us willing to undergo anything for them. Faith will bring our souls into such subjection unto the authority of Christ as Head of the church and Lord over the whole creation that we will not be terrified with what man can do unto us. Faith will furnish us with examples of the saints of God, whom he has helped and assisted to go through sufferings and who are now crowned and at rest in heaven. Faith will help us to keep our eye fixed, not upon the things of this world, but upon the eternal recompense of another world and glory therein. And faith will also work by patience when difficulties shall be multiplied upon us.

"So faith comes from

hearing, and hearing

through the word of Christ."

ROMANS 10:17

FOUR

*The Use of Faith Under
Anti-Christian Rulers*

Our inquiry is how we may live by faith with reference unto those difficulties we have or may have to struggle with in the days wherein we live. The last head we spoke to was how we may live by faith in reference to all the reproaches and scornful contempt that are cast upon that way of worship. That order and fellowship of the gospel which we cleave unto and the persecutions which we may undergo upon that account. The second difficulty that we have or may have to struggle with is the return of Popery into this land. Half the talk of the world is upon this subject. I have nothing to say to some among ourselves, but I truly believe that those who have the conduct of the papal, antichristian affairs throughout the world are endeavouring to bring it in upon us. I remember what holy Latimer said when he came to die, "Once I believed Popery would never return into England; but," he said, "I find it was not faith but fancy." I wish it would prove not so with many of us. Now, that which I am to speak unto is how we should live by faith both in the prospect of the danger of it and if it should come upon us. I will name unto you a few things which I exercise myself with. If you have more supporting thoughts and a better guidance of light, I pray God confirm it unto you.

Faith Provides Comfort During Suffering

The first thing I would exercise my thoughts upon and that my faith rests in, is that there is a fixed, determinate time in the counsel of God when Antichrist and Babylon, idolatry and superstition together with that profaneness of life which they have brought in will be destroyed. It is so fixed that it cannot be altered. All the wisdom of men, all the sins of men, and all our unbelief will not hinder it even one day. It will assuredly come to pass in its appointed season. This time is reckoned up in Scripture by days, by months, and by years. Not that we should know the time of it but that we should know the certainty of it. For if it has but so many days, but so many months, and but so many years then it must have a certain period.

Under the Old Testament we see this all along. God said to Abraham, "Know for certain that your offspring will be sojourners in a land that is not theirs and will be servants there, and they will be afflicted for four hundred years. But I will bring judgment on the nation that they serve" (Gen. 15:13–14). They did not know the beginning nor the ending of this four hundred years, but they knew that at the end of them it should be as God had said. He promised, "At the end of 430 years, on that very day, all the hosts of the Lord went out from the land of Egypt" (Ex. 12:41). Likewise, God threatens the Jews with seventy-years captivity in Babylon: "This whole land shall become a ruin and a waste, and these nations shall serve the king of Babylon seventy years. Then after seventy years are completed, I will punish the king of Babylon and that nation, the land of the Chaldeans, for their iniquity, declares the Lord" (Jer. 25:11–12).

The church did not know when they began or when they would end but they knew that the same day they were accomplished it should be as God had said and it was so. The fixing and computing of the time of the Man of Sin, of Antichrist by days, and months, and years is to secure our faith in the punctual determination of the season but not to satisfy our curiosity when the season should be. However, the consideration that there is such a time, or a determinate season is a great foundation of faith and patience. "The least one shall become a clan, and the smallest one a mighty nation; I am the Lord; in its time I will hasten it" (Isa. 60:22). If there be a fixed time for the

FAITH

accomplishment of this promise, you may ask, "How can it then be hastened?" Why, if you live in the exercise of faith and patience it will surprise you. It will come when you do not think it will nor expect it to: "In its time I will hasten it" (Isa. 60:22). I will not bring it before its time. Be you ever so patient or impatient but exercise faith and patience and I will so order it that it will be a sweet surprisal unto you.

This is actually a means of patience, "For still the vision awaits its appointed time; it hastens to the end—it will not lie. If it seems slow, wait for it; it will surely come; it will not delay" (Hab. 2:3). When we know it will come, when we know there is such a determinate time, and that it will surely come it is a great ground of patience to wait for it. This is a great consideration with me, and I leave it with you. Here I can exercise faith without fancy or conjecture that there is a certain determinate time in the counsel of God wherein he will pour out all his judgments and plagues upon the antichristian world. Anti-Christianism will be destroyed and rooted out.

Another thing that comforts my heart is that it is no less glorious to suffer under the beast and the false prophet than it was to suffer under the dragon. The book of the Revelation is chiefly made up of these two things. First, of the persecutions of the church. One by the dragon and he is conquered. The other by the beast and false prophet and they will be conquered. It was a glorious thing to suffer under that power of the dragon. Of those that did it is said, "These are the ones coming out of the great tribulation. They have washed their robes and made them white in the blood of the Lamb. Therefore, they are before the throne of God, and serve him day and night in his temple; and he who sits on the throne will shelter them with his presence" (Rev. 7:14–15). And of those that suffered under the beast and the false prophet it is said, "And they have conquered him by the blood of the Lamb and by the word of their testimony" (Rev. 12:11). We account them great and glorious people who won the liberty of the gospel and the Christian religion by suffering against the pagan power and who destroyed all idolatry by their blood, starving, and famishing all the gods of the earth (Zeph. 2:11). Never were men more glorious than they. These made up the company who, with palms in their hands and a new song in their mouths, give glory unto God (Rev. 7:9–12). I say it is not less glorious to suffer under the beast and false prophet, the second persecuting power, that is antichristian power, than it was before under paganism. The church has battled with this for many ages and must continue to do so until the time is come when they will have a perfect and complete triumph over this also. It is a glorious thing, and I would have you think upon it as such. If God shall call us to that fiery trial or any other, whatever it may be, remember that to suffer against Antichrist is as great and glorious as to suffer against Paganism.

FAITH

Though our persons fall our cause will be as truly, certainly, and infallibly victorious as that Christ sits at the right hand of God. Among the heathens, men of courage did not value their own lives and so their cause was carried on. Now, however your persons or my person may fall in this trial yet the cause in which we are engaged shall as surely conquer as Christ is alive and shall prevail at last. Upon the first rise of the beast, it is said that, "It was allowed to make war on the saints and to conquer them" (Rev. 13:7). The poor Waldenses looked upon themselves to be the people prophesied of there and said when they were under the butcheries of the papal power, "We are the conquered people of God; but there shall come forth conquerors." When going to die they knew and believed their cause would conquer. And so, after Antichrist has conquered and prevailed over people for a season, at length it will come to an end. "They will make war on the Lamb, and the Lamb will conquer them, for he is Lord of lords and King of kings, and those with him are called and chosen and faithful" (Rev. 17:14). The gospel will be victorious. This is the third thing that greatly comforts and refreshes me. That if God should give me the honor, the strength, and the grace to die in this cause, my cause will be victorious. As sure as if I had the crown in my hand.

The judgments of God will come upon the antichristian world when they do not look for them. When the kings of the earth do not look for them. Yea, when believers themselves do not look for them they will come so suddenly. The Holy Ghost says so expressly, "Her plagues will come in a single day, death and mourning and famine, and she will be burned up with fire" (Rev. 18:8). How is it possible that one that is in the state and condition she is in should have her plagues come upon her in one day? The reason is added, "For mighty is the Lord God who has judged her" (Rev. 18:8). Almighty strength will be put forth for the accomplishing of it. And if this were not enough the seventeenth verse tells you that it will come "in a single hour" (Rev. 18:17). I do truly believe that the destruction of this cursed antichristian state (of the head of it) will be brought about by none of those means we see or know of but that the strong Lord God will break in upon her and destroy her by ways unknown to us. It may be tomorrow, or it may not be in these hundred years, but when it is done, she herself will look for no such thing. "She glorified herself and lived in luxury, so give her a like measure of torment and mourning, since in her heart she says, 'I sit as a queen, I am no widow, and mourning I shall never see.' For this reason, her plagues will come in a single day" (Rev. 18:7–8). When she is boasting herself, destruction will come. When the kings of the earth will have no expectation of it for, they will cry, "Alas, alas, for the great city" that mighty city; "For in a single hour all this wealth has been laid waste" (Rev. 18:16–17). And believers themselves will be such as the children of Israel in

FAITH

Egypt when Moses came. They could not believe because of the cruel bondage they were under. It is like the day when God's judgments will come upon Antichrist, the old enemies of Jesus Christ.

I would consider very much with myself the greatness of the indignation of God against those that will comply in the least with Anti-Christianism when it does come upon us. In Revelation thirteen there is mention of a beast that had two horns like a lamb and it spoke like a dragon and he exercises all the power of the first beast (Rev. 13:11-12). That is, he exercises a power answerable to the pagan power. And what then? "Also it causes all, both small and great, both rich and poor, both free and slave, to be marked on the right hand or the forehead, so that no one can buy or sell unless he has the mark" (Rev. 13:16-17). No matter what the mark is but to receive any thing of him is to receive his mark either in our foreheads where we will show it unto all the world or in our right hands more privately where it may be shown when opportunity serves.

What then? "Then I saw another angel flying directly overhead, with an eternal gospel to proclaim to those who dwell on earth, to every nation and tribe and language and people. And he said with a loud voice, Fear God and give him glory, because the hour of his judgment has come, and worship him who made heaven and earth, the sea and the springs of water" (Rev. 14:6–7). When Antichrist would bring his mark on the foreheads of the people and

Steadfast in Trials

into their hands, God, by his gospel, calls men from their false worship and idolatry. But what if they do not obey? The verses tell us, "Another angel, a third, followed them, saying with a loud voice, "If anyone worships the beast and its image and receives a mark on his forehead or on his hand, he also will drink the wine of God's wrath, poured full strength into the cup of his anger, and he will be tormented with fire and sulfur in the presence of the holy angels and in the presence of the Lamb" (Rev. 14:9–10). Some will be apt to say, "Let us make a fair composition and use some compliance to put an end to these disputes." No, do it at your peril. God says you will drink of the wine of his wrath which is poured out without mixture into the cup of his indignation and that for ever and ever. And I believe with all my heart and soul that this will be the portion of all the men and women in this nation that will comply with any return of antichristian idolatry among us. God will pour out his indignation upon them.

Remember that if the trial comes it is a day of battle and it is not for you when you should just engage in a battle to be considering of this or that way or contrivance to escape. No, it is courage, constancy, and faith alone that must be set on work or you will not be preserved. All your wisdom and contrivances will not preserve you. But it being come to the issue between Christ and Antichrist it is the girding up the loins of your mind and a resisting unto blood against sin and abiding in it that is your duty and must preserve you. Nothing will save you but faith, courage, and constancy.

There are insinuations in the Scripture that those who in a special manner cleave unto God and his worship with faith, love, and delight will be preserved and saved. I do not propose this unto you as an object of your faith. All the rest I do but I say there are intimations that give me some satisfaction. That they who with quick and lively spirits do act in faith, love, and delight in God and his worship or that are worshippers in the inner court of the temple, will be peculiarly secured at such a time. But I am afraid few of us will have it because I see so much coldness and deadness grown generally upon us and the churches of Christ. It makes me think exercises will come upon us all for we have need of them.

To conclude, first, let not your talk about strange things keep the thoughts of these things you have been hearing out of your hearts. For you will be tried with Anti-Christianism before you die. We talk of news, of the great things we look for in the world, and that Antichrist will be destroyed and so he will, but I do believe he will try us sorely in the meantime. Second, take heed of predictions. How woefully and wretchedly we have been mistaken by this! We know the time is determined. Its beginning and ending are known to God and we must live by faith till the accomplishment. Third, so many of us as have engaged ourselves afresh in covenant unto God, let us remember that we have taken the mark of God upon our foreheads and it will ill become us to set the mark of Antichrist by it. This is all I have to offer unto you about living by faith under the apprehensions of those difficulties we must struggle with in reference to the coming in of profaneness and idolatry. With which we are threatened by hell and the world which are at this day combining to bring them again upon this nation.

"Without faith it is impossible to please him, for whoever would draw near to God must believe that he exists and that he rewards those who seek him."

HEBREWS 11:6

FIVE

The Use of Faith in a Time of General Decline

I have now come to the last thing that was proposed to be spoken about and with which I will close the subject. How we may live by faith under an apprehension of great and woeful decays in churches, in church-members, in professors of all sorts, and in the gradual withdrawing of the glory of God from us all on that account.

I would speak unto three things: 1. That this is such a time of decay among us, among churches, among church-members, and professors of all sorts and ways throughout this nation and other nations too, and where there are any that fear God. 2. That this is and ought to be a cause of great trouble and trial unto all that are true believers. 3. I will show you how we may live by faith in such a season and what it is faith will do to support the soul at such a time. There are too many signs that show it is now such a time of decay but I will name a few.

The Evidence of Decay Among Us

A sense of it is impressed upon the minds of all the most discerning and diligent Christians that do abound most in self-examination or do take most notice of the ways of God. I have heard multitudes testifying of it. Complaints are received from many in this nation and the neighboring nations that there is a great decay in the power of grace and life of faith among all sorts of professors and some of them will go farther in their evidence and tell us that they find the effects of it in themselves. That they find it a matter of great difficulty and requiring great watchfulness and great diligence to keep up themselves in any measure unto their former frames and when they have done all they do not attain their desire. And to increase this evidence we are all convinced of it or else we are notorious hypocrites. For I do not know how often I have heard it prayed over in this very place. So that there is a conviction from God sent forth upon the hearts and minds of spiritual and self-examining believers that churches, church-members, professors, and themselves are under spiritual decays. This is the first evidence. Therefore, in such a season, it was the best part of the church that made that sad complaint, "O Lord, why do you make us wander from your ways and harden our heart, so that we fear you not" (Isa. 63:17)? They were conscious that there was a judgment of the hand of God upon them.

The open lack of love that is among churches, church-members, and professors is another evidence of decay. I will not speak of the lack of love among churches one to another but as to love among church-members. We have scarce the shadow of it remaining among us. Where men have relations, where they have acquaintance, where they have been old friends, where they agree in humor and converse, and where they agree in a party and faction there is an appearance of love. But upon the pure spiritual account of Christianity and church-membership we have scarce the shadow of it left among us. I remember how it was with us when it was a joy of heart to behold the face of one another. Where there was love without dissimulation and in sincerity. Love attended with pity, compassion, humility, and delight but it is dead in churches and dead among professors.

Another evidence of this decay is the lack of delight and diligence in the ordinances of gospel worship. These ordinances used to be a joy of heart unto all that feared God but now there is so much deadness, coldness, and indifference. So much undervaluing of the word, so much fulness of self, pride, and an apprehension that we know everything. So little endeavour to tremble at every truth by what means soever it be brought unto us as gives a manifest evidence of woeful decays that have fallen upon us. Dead preachers and dead hearers! All things now go down among the churches of God and professors in these nations. This is attended with two desperate evils.

One of which I heard only recently (but upon inquiry I find it to be a far greater evil than I took it to be). Namely, men under an apprehension that they do not see others enlivened nor quickened as they used to be by the ordinances of divine worship and finding no such thing in their own hearts either (in all probability finding themselves to grow dead and useless) are fallen into an opinion that there is an end of them and that they ought to attend unto them no more. And this happens to some that have long walked soberly and with great diligence in the use of ordinances. Some in this city and in other places are led by foolish delusions to it because they do not find the spirit, and life, and power of the word and ordinances in themselves and, as they think, in others. A godly and learned minister that showed me a discourse written upon this subject in defence of ordinances did acquaint me with so great a number falling into this abomination that I did not think it had been possible.

The other evil that attends it is that this deadness and indifferency unto ordinances and a lack of bringing our necks to the yoke of Christ therein against all disputes and arguments of flesh and blood has taken such place among us and went so far that all ways of reformation are useless.

Men may make divisions and I do not know what but this I know that there is no way of obtaining any reformation but for men to engage their hearts to return unto God in more delight in his service than there has been. Some utterly forsake the assemblies. Some come with great indifference, using their liberty, off and on, at their pleasure. Are not these things evidences of great decays among us? To me they are. I speak not as to the state of all churches that I know or can hear of in these nations.

The last evidence I will mention of these decays among us is our worldly-mindedness. Our conformity to the world and security. These things have been so often spoken to you and no reformation has ensued that now they are looked upon as words of course and I am discouraged from speaking of them anymore. But assure yourselves that this conformity to the world and this security that is yet found among us is a great evidence that the glory of God is departing from us. Ministers preach against worldly-mindedness, security, etc., but it makes no impression upon the minds of men. For we can scarce give an instance in any of the least reformation. These things plainly demonstrate that we are all under great decays. A sense of this general decay among churches, church- members, and professors, ought to be an exercise and concern unto our minds. If we think all is well with us and are satisfied while we are free from outward troubles and do not concern ourselves about our decays, I will not say we are hypocrites but, truly we are poor, low, dead, carnal, and unspiritual Christians.

Suppose it be this way and we do complain of it to one another, not knowing what the issue will be nor what it may come unto. How will we live by faith under this consideration? What is the work of faith in this condition? If things are so (and I wish anyone could show that they are not; but suppose that they are so) and our souls are burdened with an apprehension that they are so, then what will faith do to enable us to pass through this exercise and to live unto God? I will tell you something of what I find and if God does not help you to better things then make use of these and improve them so that you may give glory to God by believing under this condition also.

The Sustaining Work of Faith

Faith will mind the soul that notwithstanding this also, yet Christ has built his church upon that rock and that it will not be utterly prevailed against. The promise says faith extends itself as well to the inbred adversaries of our own souls, unbelief, deadness, and all these things as to our outward enemies. "On this rock I will build my church, and the gates of hell shall not prevail against it" (Matt. 16:18). Though we were all dead, helpless, lifeless, poor creatures and though we had retained almost nothing but outward order and had lost the very vigour and essence of faith and obedience, yet Christ's church shall abide and stand and those that belong to him shall be preserved. Such and such are turned apostates, yet the apostle says, "But God's firm foundation stands, bearing this seal: The Lord knows those who are his" (2 Tim. 2:19). Here is my ground of hope, notwithstanding all this, though one falls after another, though one decays after another, "God's firm foundation stands" and it has a seal upon it, "The Lord knows those who are his" (2 Tim. 2:19). Everyone whom he has effectually called and built upon the rock, Jesus Christ, will be preserved whatever befalls the residue of the world. To see such a convergence of all manner of dangerous evils from without as are coming this day upon the church of God and to see, in the meantime, so many signs of a decaying spiritual state in believers themselves it will put faith to exercise itself upon this promise of Christ, who declared, "On this rock I will build my church; and the gates of hell shall not prevail against it" (Matt. 16:18). If you find your spirits at any time pressed with these things, if nothing better occurs at hand, exercise faith upon this promise of Christ and upon the firm standing of the foundation of God, that he knows who are his and will carry them through all these difficulties and land them safe in eternity.

Faith will also mind the soul that God has yet the fulness and residue of the Spirit and can pour it out when he pleases to recover us from this woeful state and condition and to renew us to holy obedience unto himself. There are more promises of God's giving supplies of his Spirit to deliver us from inward decays than there are for the use of the acts of his power to deliver us from our outward enemies. God is as able to do the inward work, to revive and renew a spirit of faith, love, holiness, meekness, humility, self-denial, and readiness for the cross. He is able with one word and act of his grace to renew it as he is able by one act of his power to destroy all his enemies and make them the footstool of Christ when he pleases. Live in the faith of this.

The psalmist says, "He scatters frost like ashes" (Ps. 147:16–17), and the issue is that the earth is frozen. He brings a death upon it but he says, "When you send forth your Spirit, they are created, and you renew the face of the ground" (Ps. 104:30). In like manner there is deadness upon all churches and professors in some measure at this time but God, who has the fulness of the Spirit, can send him forth and renew the face of the soul. He can give professors and profession another face. Not to trim and trick as now so often is done. Not so high, and haughty, not so earthly, and worldly, as is now so much seen but humble, meek, holy, broken-hearted, and self-denying. God can send forth his Spirit when he pleases and give all our churches and professors a new face in the richness and flourishing of his grace in them. When God will do this, I do not know but I believe God can do this and that he is able to do it! Able to renew all his churches by sending out supplies of the Spirit, whose fulness is with him, to recover them in the due and appointed time. And more I truly believe that when God has accomplished some ends upon us and has stained the glory of all flesh, he will renew the power and glory of religion among us again, even in this nation. I believe it truly but not as I believe the other things that I have mentioned unto you. For those I believe absolutely. Namely, that Christ has built his church upon a rock and that nothing shall ever finally prevail against it. That God has the fulness and the residue of the Spirit to renew us again to all the glory of profession and holy obedience. These I propose as truths that are infallible, that will not fail you, and upon which you may venture your souls to eternity. And if your faith will not give you support and comfort in these things, I do not know what else will.

When your souls are perplexed within you about these things your faith will say unto you, O my soul, why are you cast down? Are not all these things foretold thee? "That in later times some will depart from the faith" (1 Tim. 4:1). "But understand this, that in the last days there will come times of difficulty" because of those "Having the appearance of godliness but denying its power" (2 Tim. 3:1–5). Has it not been foretold that churches will decay and lose their first faith and love in examples that have been set before you? Why are you surprised? Asks our Savior, "I have said these things to you, that when their hour comes you may remember that I told them to you" (John 16:4). I was never nearer a surprise than by this one thing. How it could possibly be that after so many instructions, after so many mercies, trials, fears, so many years carrying our lives in our hands, and so many glorious deliverances there should still be decays found amongst us and such going backward. It is a great surprise to one that considers it a right but seeing it is foretold that it will be so, let us live by faith. God has some great end to accomplish out of it and then all will be well. "When the Lord has finished all his work on Mount Zion and on Jerusalem, he will punish the speech of the arrogant heart of the king of Assyria and the boastful look in his eyes" (Isa. 10:12).

Last, faith if it be in exercise will put every soul in whom it is upon an especial attendance unto those duties God calls him unto in such a season. This accomplishes and completes our living by faith under such a trial as this is. If faith be in us and in exercise it will put us upon all these duties that God requires of us in such a season. It will put us upon self-examination to determine how far we are engaged in these decays ourselves and have contracted the guilt of them. It will put us in great mourning because of God's withdrawing himself from us. It will put us upon watchfulness over ourselves and over one another that we be not overtaken by the means and causes of these decays. It will give us zeal for God and the honor of the gospel that it may not suffer by reason of our shortcomings.

In a word, faith will do something but for our parts we do little or nothing. Faith will do something wherever it is when it is stirred up to exercise but as to these special duties in reference to these decays that all professors are fallen under, O how little we do in any kind whatsoever! We might discuss with one another what to do under these decays to further one another in recovering ourselves from them! This then is what we are called to and what is required of us. Namely, faith in the faithfulness of Christ who has built his church upon the rock so that even if these things are ever so bad it will not be prevailed against. Faith in the fulness of the Spirit and his promise to send him to renew the face of the church, faith in apprehending the truth of God who has foretold these things, and faith putting us upon those special duties that God requires at our hands in such a season.

www.ingramcontent.com/pod-product-compliance
Lightning Source LLC
Chambersburg PA
CBHW072206100526
44589CB00015B/2392